HILLARY CLINTON

by Stephanie Fitzgerald

Content Consultant

Nanci R. Vargus, Ed.D.
Professor Emeritus, University of Indianapolis

Reading Consultant

Jeanne M. Clidas, Ph.D.
Reading Specialist

Children's Press®
An Imprint of Scholastic Inc.

Library of Congress Cataloging-in-Publication Data
A CIP catalog record for this book is available from the Library of Congress.
ISBN 9780531229316 (library binding) | ISBN 9780531234068 (pbk.)

Produced by Spooky Cheetah Press
Design by Judith Christ-Lafond
Poem by Jodie Shepherd

Printed in the United States of America   113

SCHOLASTIC, CHILDREN'S PRESS, ROOKIE BIOGRAPHIES™, and associated logos are trademarks and/or registered trademarks of Scholastic Inc.

1 2 3 4 5 6 7 8 9 10 R 26 25 24 23 22 21 20 19 18 17

Photographs ©: cover: Lucas Jackson/Reuters/Alamy Images; cover red ribbon: AliceLiddelle/iStockphoto; back cover: Igor Shikov/Shutterstock, Inc.; 3: spawns/iStockphoto; 4-5: Justin Sullivan/Getty Images; 7 top left: Polaris Images; 7 maps: Mapping Specialists; 8: Courtesy of the William J. Clinton Presidential Library; 9: Rue des Archives/The Granger Collection; 11: Charles Dixon/Boston Globe/Getty Images; 12: Mike Stewart/Sygma/Getty Images; 14 bottom: Courtesy of the William J. Clinton Presidential Library; 14-15 main: Mike Stewart/Sygma/Getty Images; 16: Barbara Kinney/White House/The LIFE Picture Collection/Getty Images; 19: Stephen Jaffe/AFP/Getty Images; 20-21: Michael Appleton/NY Daily News Archive/Getty Images; 22-23: Kevin Lamarque/Reuters; 24: Evan Vucci/AFP/Getty Images; 26-27 main: Zach D Roberts/NurPhoto/Getty Images; 27 top right: Evan Vucci/AP Images; 29: Kathy Willens-Pool/Getty Images; 30: Orhan Cam/Shutterstock, Inc.; 31 center top: Matthew Ragen/Thinkstock; 31 center bottom: Per-Anders Pettersson/Getty Images; 31 top: Charles Dixon/Boston Globe/Getty Images; 31 bottom: Michael Appleton/NY Daily News Archive/Getty Images; 32: Orhan Cam/Shutterstock, Inc.

Maps by Mapping Specialists

Sources:
page 13: Clinton, Hillary. *Living History*, NY Simon & Schuster, 2003. page 30
page 26: CNN accessed at http://www.cnn.com/videos/politics/2016/07/28/dnc-convention-obama-never-a-man-or-woman-more-qualified-than-hillary-sot.cnn

TABLE OF CONTENTS

Meet Hillary Rodham Clinton 5

Choosing Her Path 10

Taking Charge............................. 18

Looking to the Future 26

A Poem About Hillary Clinton 30

You Can Be a Leader...................... 30

Glossary 31

Index 32

Facts for Now 32

About the Author 32

Meet Hillary Rodham Clinton

From the time she was a little girl, Hillary Rodham Clinton worked to help others. She spent her life fighting to give people better lives. In 2016, she was the first woman ever to run for U.S. president as head of a major political party.

Hillary Diane Rodham was born on October 26, 1947, in Chicago, Illinois. She and her two younger brothers grew up in nearby Park Ridge.

The Rodhams had everything they needed. Hillary's mother showed her that some people were not as lucky. She taught Hillary to help others.

FAST FACT!

Hillary was a Girl Scout. She earned lots of merit badges!

Hillary (center) poses with her parents and her brother Hugh.

CANADA

NEW YORK

Chicago ●

UNITED STATES

■ ILLINOIS

■ WASHINGTON, D.C.

■ ARKANSAS

MEXICO

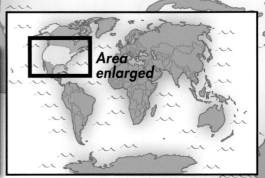

Area enlarged

MAP KEY

● City where Hillary Clinton was born

■ Places where Hillary Clinton lived

This is Hillary when she was about 13 years old.

In elementary school, Hillary organized carnivals to raise money for charity. She collected clothes for poor families. She was a straight-A student, too. Hillary also liked to have fun. She and her friends played football, went ice-skating, and rode bikes together.

In high school, Hillary was voted "Most Likely to Succeed."

Choosing Her Path

In 1965, Hillary started at Wellesley College. She knew she wanted to make a difference in the world. Hillary entered Yale Law School after college. She decided to focus her studies on children's rights.

FAST FACT!

In 1969, Hillary made a speech at her college graduation. It was the first time a student ever spoke at Wellesley's **commencement**.

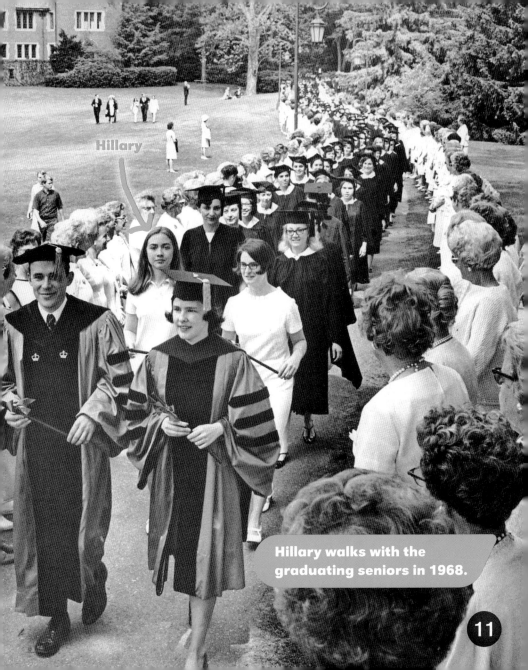

Hillary

Hillary walks with the graduating seniors in 1968.

Hillary has always spoken out about important issues.

In 1971, Hillary met Yale classmate Bill Clinton.
He was from Arkansas.

In the summer of 1973, Hillary worked for the Children's Defense Fund. The CDF helps children living in **poverty**.

FAST FACT!

"I realized that what I wanted to do with the law was to give voice to children who were not being heard."
— Hillary Clinton

13

Hillary graduated from law school. About a year later, she moved to Arkansas. She became a law professor. In 1975, she and Bill were married.

Three years later, Bill was elected governor of Arkansas. On February 27, 1980, the Clintons' daughter, Chelsea, was born.

Here are Hillary and Bill on their wedding day.

Hillary, Bill, and Chelsea wave to spectators during a parade.

Hillary and Chelsea visit an orphanage in India.

Bill's political career continued to grow. In 1992, he was elected president of the United States. When he took office, Hillary became First Lady.

As First Lady, Hillary visited more than 80 countries. Chelsea often traveled with her mother. In some countries, girls are thought to be less important than boys. Hillary wanted others to see how important girls really are.

Taking Charge

Bill was president for two terms. After that, the Clintons moved to New York.

In 2000, Hillary was elected senator from New York. She soon faced a big challenge. On September 11, 2001, **terrorists** attacked New York City. Clinton helped the city recover.

Clinton is elected the first female senator from New York.

Clinton visits with marines in Iraq.

Clinton was a popular senator. She was re-elected in 2006. Senator Clinton focused on several issues. She fought to get good health care for **veterans**. She worked to make sure every child could get a good education.

FAST FACT!

Clinton puts hot sauce on all her food—even salad!

In 2008, President Barack Obama named Clinton secretary of state. She handled the United States' relationships with other countries. Secretary Clinton visited 112 countries.

Secretary Clinton worked closely with President Obama.

23

Clinton visits girls living
in a shelter in Cambodia.

24

Secretary Clinton traveled to a lot of poor countries. In some places, children cannot go to school. They can die from illnesses that could be easily cured. Clinton worked to improve the lives of the people she met.

FAST FACT!

The Clintons' first granddaughter was born in 2014. Her name is Charlotte. In 2016, they welcomed grandson Aidan.

Looking to the Future

In 2016, Clinton ran for president. President Obama said, "There has never been a man or a woman...who is more qualified to be president than Hillary Clinton." Many Americans agreed. In the end, Clinton lost to Donald Trump.

Clinton's opponent was businessman Donald Trump.

What will Hillary Clinton do next? It is hard to say. One thing is for sure, though. She will continue to fight to make sure everyone in America has a chance at a great life.

Timeline of Hillary Clinton's Life

1947 > **1975** > **1980**

Born on October 26

Marries Bill Clinton

Daughter, Chelsea, born

Re-elected to Senate

Runs for president

2000 > **2006** > **2008** > **2016**

Elected senator
from New York

Named secretary
of state

A Poem About Hillary Clinton

So many ways she's served our nation—
Hillary worked hard for education,
and health care, and equal rights for all.
Public service is her call.

You Can Be a Leader

 Work hard in school and learn as much as you can about the world around you.

 Find something you believe in and fight for it.

 Never let anyone make you doubt your dreams or abilities!

Glossary

commencement (kuh-MENS-muhnt): graduation ceremony

poverty (PAH-vur-tee): the state of being poor

terrorists (TER-ur-ists): people who use violence and threats to get others to obey

veterans (VET-ur-uhnz): people who have served in the armed forces, especially during a war

Index

Children's Defense Fund............................ **13**

Clinton, Bill........**13, 14, 17, 18**

Clinton, Chelsea............... **14, 17**

college........................ **10**

early life................. **6–8**

First Lady.................... **17**

law school.... **10, 13,14**

Obama, Barack.................**22, 26**

president **5, 26**

professor **14**

secretary of state **22–25**

senator............... **18–21**

Trump, Donald **26**

Facts for Now

Visit this Scholastic Web site for more information on Hillary Clinton and download the Teaching Guide for this series:

www.factsfornow.scholastic.com

Enter the keywords Hillary Clinton

About the Author

Stephanie Fitzgerald, who has written many nonfiction books for young readers, loves to read and tries to learn something new every day. She hopes to one day cast her vote for the first female U.S. president.